Eastern Heart Vocabulary
seeing you meeting you

by

W.M.Aslam

First published © 2016
This copy revised © 2020

Contents

Author's Introduction	06
I'm Saira	09
Oh, Beautiful One	11
When I Saw You	13
Oh, Love Come Now	15
What Happened To My Heart?	17
Take Me Away From Here	19
On Seeing You I Fell In Love	21
This Heart Is So Crazy	23
What Are You Going To Do?	25
The Season Of Love	27
I Saw You I Wanted You	29
Our Hearts Are Rusting In Time	31
You're A Part Of My Daily Life	33
Tomorrow May Or May Not Come	35
Only Ever You	37
Seeing You Meeting You	39
Heart Of Mine	41
Something's Starting To Happen	43
I Am Your True Love	45
My Heart	47
Day And Night	49
Silence Of My Heart	51
Come Out	53
Always Missing Each Other	55
Now I Know Real Love	57
What Do I Do Now?	59
Raja And Rani	61
My Heart Can't Stop Crying	63
A Heart Among Weeping Flowers	65

Sunita And Her Love	67
Don't Change Like The Weather	69
The Day We Stop Loving Life	71
A Day Without Words	73
Slowly	75
Your Name	77
These Are Our Times	79
Say – Say – Say	81
A Week Without You	83
Do You Still Remember?	85
Iron Heart	87
My Dear Life	89
Tell Me	91
Your Face	93
I Don't Need It	95
The Trials of Life	97
I'll Be Your Vice	99
Useless	101
Away	103
Trust	105
Not Twice	107
Dreams	109
Eternal	111
Still	113
Rain	115
I'd Fallen	117
I Love You	119
A Part Of My Daily Life	121
Fragrance	123
Unhide	125

Faults	127
Nothing's The Same	129
Flowers	131
Thanks To You	133
Deep	135
Star Crossed	137
The Night A Meeting Occurred	139
In The Ticking of My Watch	141
It Takes A Third To Unite Lovers	143
Broken Pieces	145
Hide	147

Author's Introduction

I decided to put together this collection of rhyme and prose for two reasons, firstly to caution those who play with love, and secondly, to show the value of love to those who have been blessed with it.

We live in what I have come to view as the *Disposable Age*. From disposable shavers to disposable gloves, and disposable marriages to disposable kids. This may shock you, but you only have to read the news to see how our *throw away* mentality has entered so many spheres of our lives. What happened to the sacredness of love? Has love also become *disposable*?

We can't expect a broken heart to contain love. It's like mending a cracked eggshell or piece of fine porcelain, sure you can put it back together, but the cracks will always remain.

Don't betray a friend or partner. Don't break their trust. When trust has gone it can never be fully repaired. Doubts will seep into the hairline cracks no matter how hard you try to patch things up.

Take my advice, be honest and open with love, it won't hurt anyone that way, failure to do so will inevitably corrupt your own heart and leave you unloved. For those who have lost love and are in pain, don't worry, it will soon pass. You will live to love again. The heart is able to self-heal over time. The medicine is in the pain.

If you feel like crying whilst reading these poems, do so freely, and let nothing stop you. Crying is known to be a great therapy, whereas holding back tears is detrimental to both mind and body. It is a dead heart that no longer weeps.

If you are among the lucky ones who have found the love you sought, I encourage you to do all that you can to keep and protect it. Never let anyone interfere with or come between your love. Never.

- W.M.Aslam

8

I'm Saira

I'm Saira, I'm Saira
This is who I am, this is all of me
Whoever lays their eyes on me
Whoever hears my voice
They'll want to meet me.

Saira, oh Saira, you are so beautiful
I am, I am
Saira, oh Saira, they all want to meet you
They do, they do.

Whoever sees me will want no other
I'll love him as my first love
Whoever that man might be
He'll surely want to meet me.

I'm Saira, I'm Saira
This is who I am, this is all of me
Whoever lays their eyes on me
Whoever hears my voice
They'll definitely want to meet me.

Saira, oh Saira, you are so wonderful
I am, I am
Saira, oh Saira, they are all crazy about you
They are, they are.

I'm Saira, I'm Saira
Searching for my true love
Wandering day and night
For that man who I'll one day meet.

Oh, Beautiful One

Oh, beautiful one
When the stars appear you out-dazzle them
Oh, splendid one
When the sun rises you outshine it
Oh, romantic one
Flowers bloom in vain to compete with your beauty
Oh, delicate one
The birds sing unable to match your voice
Oh, charming one
Diamonds can't sparkle as bright
Oh, precious one
Gold can't match your allure
One day I'll win your heart
Until then - I'll watch you from afar.

12

When I Saw You

When I saw you, I knew it was true love
Love had been granted from Heaven above
My heart no longer searched
My body no longer yearned.

My eyes could not look away
Unable to move, such was your beauty
My heart had never felt this way
I wasn't sure what to do, or say.

Now that I've seen you there is no one else
Please tell me where we go from here?
Take away these feelings of uncertainty
Tell me you feel the same way as me.

Oh, Love Come Now

Love, why won't you come to me?
When will you arrive?
There is love here, and you seek love too
Love and love make a great match, you'll agree
Oh, Love, you can come and see
After all these years take away my worries
After all these years throw out my doubts
Look at the state I have gotten myself into
Waiting and worrying for your arrival
Love, why won't you come to me?
After all these years, come and kindle my fire
Come tell me that your love sought mine.

16

What Happened To My Heart?

What happened to my heart?
It was fine just a moment ago
It wasn't until I saw you
That it began feeling like this.

What happened to my heart?
It was fine only yesterday
It wasn't until I met you
That it began to feel this way.

What happened to my heart?
There must be some explanation
Is there something about you -
that makes it feel such emotion?

18

Take Me Away From Here

Take me away from here
Hide me in your heart
I feel so alone in this world
So far from your love
Come, hold me in your arms.

*I'll come and take you away
I'm also alone my Dear
I'll hide you in my heart
I'll make your loneliness disappear
I won't let you live without love.*

Take my heart and unite it with yours
We needn't both remain alone
Come and embrace me
Let us hide away from the world.

*I will unite us my Love
We won't remain alone
I'll hide you from the world
I'll protect you from the cold.*

20

On Seeing You I Fell In Love

On seeing you I fell in love
That's just the way love unfolds
But where we go from here
No one really knows.

These eyes of mine caught hold of you
This heart of mine fell for you
But then came the uncertainty
Of which no one knows.

I prayed for my True Love
I called and you answered
But do we have a future together?
I guess no one really knows.

22

The Heart Is So Crazy

                    The heart is so crazy
                 Sometimes it makes me smile
                  Sometimes it makes me cry
                The strange thoughts it brings me
            It tells me about love and then about pain
                  Many strange dreams it shows
                  Those dreams never come true
                  So many crazy ideas it gives
                 None of them make any sense
The heart wakes up warm
Other days it feels so cold
The thoughts that come to it
Leave me so confused
Is there any cure for this heart?
Will it always be this way?
Will it ever be content?
The heart is so crazy
Sometimes it makes me smile
Sometimes it makes me cry
Giving me many sleepless nights.

24

What Are You Going To Do?

What are you going to do?
When you're feeling this blue?
Who are you going to call
When you're all alone?

Make some changes in your life
Turn back - there's still time
Go back and seek out old friends
Go back and see it's not the end.

Sitting around won't solve anything
Dial that number and give someone a ring
Don't let your pride get the better of you
It's time to end the life of a fool.

26

The Season Of Love

It is the season of love
I am here thinking of
The days we'd spent together
Our love blossomed in warmer weather.

In the season of love
I lie on the grass watching clouds above
Just like we used to back then
Back when it all first began.

In the season of love
You'll find me always on the move
Hoping I might soon find
A place to soothe this aching mind.

28

I Saw You, I Wanted You

I saw you, I wanted you
With you I fell in love
That was my only mistake
What else did I do wrong?

After all these years I still recognise you
I just ask that you come and talk to me.

I only saw you, I only wanted you
With you I fell in love
That was my only mistake
What else did I do wrong?

The mirror shows my heart breaking
It can't hide the way I feel inside.

I only saw you, I only wanted you
With you I fell in love
That was my only mistake
What else did I do wrong?

Until I find true love
I will always feel this way.

Our Hearts Are Rusting In Time

Our hearts are rusting in time
Our bodies decaying slowly
We'll only love a very short while
Love will always remain a mystery.

Our hearts are rusting in time
Each day brings further corrosion
As though sentenced for some unknown crime
Our hearts under constant subversion.

Our hearts are rusting in time
Submerged in a pool of emotions
Whether we choose to laugh or cry
None of us will make it out alive.

A Part Of My Daily Life

From the clothes you wear
To the colour of your hair
You're a part of my daily life.

From the friends you choose
To the style of your shoes
You're a part of my daily life.

From the sound of your voice
To every little choice
You're a part of my daily life.

From the colour of your skin
To whether you lose or win
You're a part of my daily life.

From the smell of your perfume
To your success or ruin
You're a part of my daily life.

From being married or single
Whether you choose to mingle
You're a part of my daily life.

Tomorrow May Or May Not Come

Every watch ticks slowly
Every heart beats softly
Tomorrow may or may not come
By sunrise some of us may be gone.

What have we left behind?
What have we sent ahead?
Is there anything to remind
As we lay lifeless in our bed?

So much love I had given
So many days I'd dealt with trouble
Was there a meaning to this life?
Are we only to live and then die?

When our presence becomes mere ashes
When that moment comes and life flashes
What will be on our mind and lips?
What will we take on that final trip?

Only Ever You

There was only ever you
You were my joy and my pain
Our relationship could never be broken
Everything in our hearts we'd spoken
It was our destiny to be together
You were my tears and my laughter
There was only ever you.

                There was only ever you
           We've been together so many years
        I couldn't imagine us ever being apart
                  From morning until night
                  We'd never be out of sight
          So blessed to have found each other
          So easy to have loved one another
                There was only ever you.

38

Seeing You, Meeting You

Seeing you, meeting you
It's been such a pleasure
I can't explain what it is about you
Every word and every gesture
Makes me feel so warm inside.

Seeing you, meeting you
You're always on my mind
I don't understand what it is about you
Every step and every smile
Makes me feel so alive inside.

Seeing you, meeting you
It's what I look forward to
I don't know what it is about you
Every walk and every talk
Makes me feel so good inside.

40

Heart Of Mine

Oh, Heart of mine, tell me why
Tell me why you fell in love?
Oh, Heart, be not shy, tell me why
Why you are so irresponsible?
You fall without any self-control
Fall in love without my consent.

Oh, Heart of mine, don't play with love
Take my advice for once
I don't think there is a thing like you
in any other creature
You fall in love without self-control
Fall in love without my knowing.

Oh, Heart of mine, l am warning you
you'll get us into trouble
You'd better start behaving yourself
I'm not prepared to bail you out
every time you fall in love
I'll lose my mind if nothing else.

42

Something's Starting To Happen

Sleepless nights
My mind elsewhere
These are the signs of first love
Something's starting to happen.

Daydreams and forgetfulness
My loss of appetite
These are the signs of feeling in love
Something's starting to happen.

Smiling to myself
My friends showing concern
These are the signs of falling in love
Something's about to happen.

44

I Am Your True Love

I am your true love
You should come and meet me
I am your true love
You should come and talk to me.

I've loved you since we first met
Neither of us will ever forget
All the things we've been through
All the dreams we've planned ahead.

I am your true love
You can come and meet me
I am your true love
You can come and talk to me.

46

My Heart

I remembered you for only a moment
What was my heart supposed to do?
It awoke - craving your love
It caused my mind to overthink.

My heart now seeks yours
What can I do if it longs -
longs to be by your side?
Sending my thoughts so wild.

My heart does what it feels
There's nothing I can do
There' nothing I can say
To stop my heart from loving you.

48

Day And Night

I weep for having lost your love
My heart neither wakes nor sleeps
I truly felt you were mine to keep
We climbed that mountain so very steep
I'd do it all again to get you back
Risk life and limb to see you again
I'll go mad sat here thinking of you
My heart unable to sleep or wake
Your memory keeps me here
Hoping you'll come back someday -
and things will be just the same
That our love will be so much more
Thinking of you my heart it weeps
Day and night it longs for you
Unable to sleep or wake -
in such a lonely place.

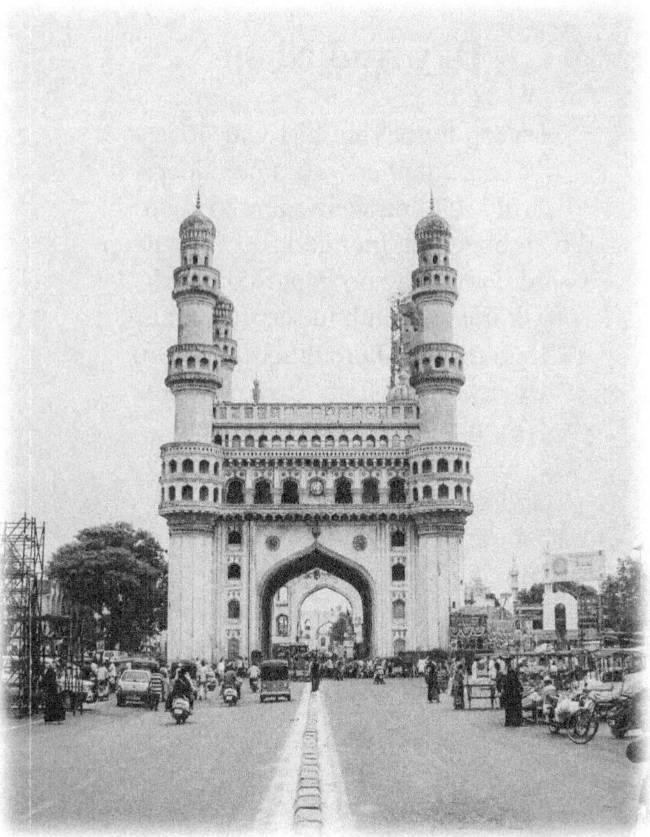

Silence Of My Heart

Through sadness and joy
My heart remains silent
Through all of the hurt and pain
It never speaks a word
All my heart knows – is silence
Hidden away out of your sight
Emotions never able to show
No one can persuade it to speak
No one will know what it conceals
Through tragedy and success
Silent - it will always remain
Never willing to reveal
What others so easily feel.

52

Come Out

Come out from my picture
Just for a little while
Come out from my dream
Let us spend some time.

Remove yourself from my thoughts
Let me see you in the flesh
Remove yourself from my mind
Come and fulfill this wish.

Step aside from my anxiety
Let us talk sweet words together
Step aside from my insecurity
Assure me we'll always be together.

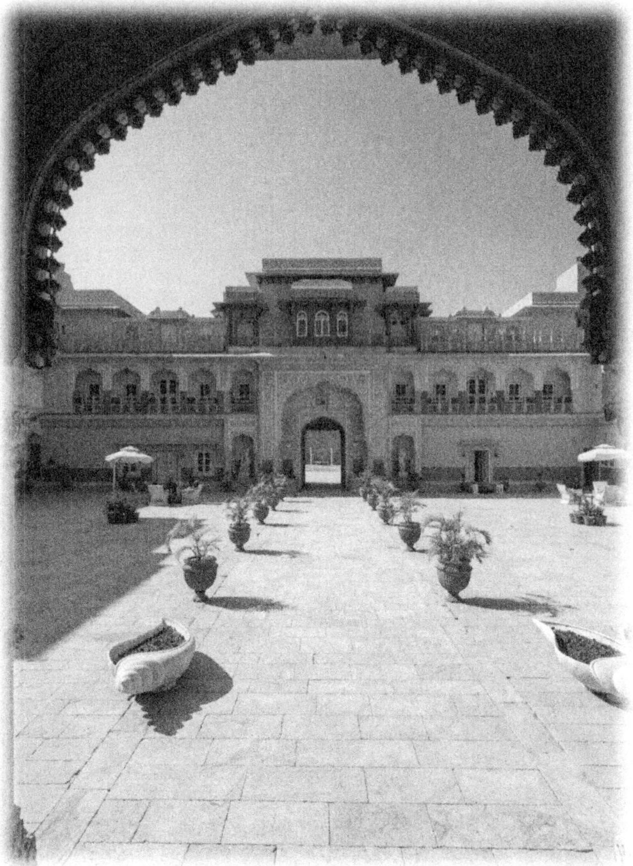

Always Missing Each Other

I am the darkness of night
You are the light of day
Always missing each other
Never able to meet.

I am the warm midday sun
You are the splendid full moon
Always missing each other
Never able to meet.

I am the early autumn
You are the late winter
Always missing each other
Never able to meet.

56

Now I know Real Love

I have realised the kind of love you wanted
The kind of love two people will die for
I was so foolish and immature
My intentions were never clear
I wish I'd known better back then
I wish I'd sung you your favourite songs.

You surprised me on my birthday
With a cake in the shape of a chocolate car
No one had done such a kind thing before
Such kindness that made me emotional
It was then that I realised what I had
How much you really knew and loved me.

Torn apart - your family never accepted me
My only option was to let you down gently
Though it broke my heart, I tried not to show it
To this day I still think well of you
Hoping you're happy wherever you are
Hoping this fool will one day find love too.

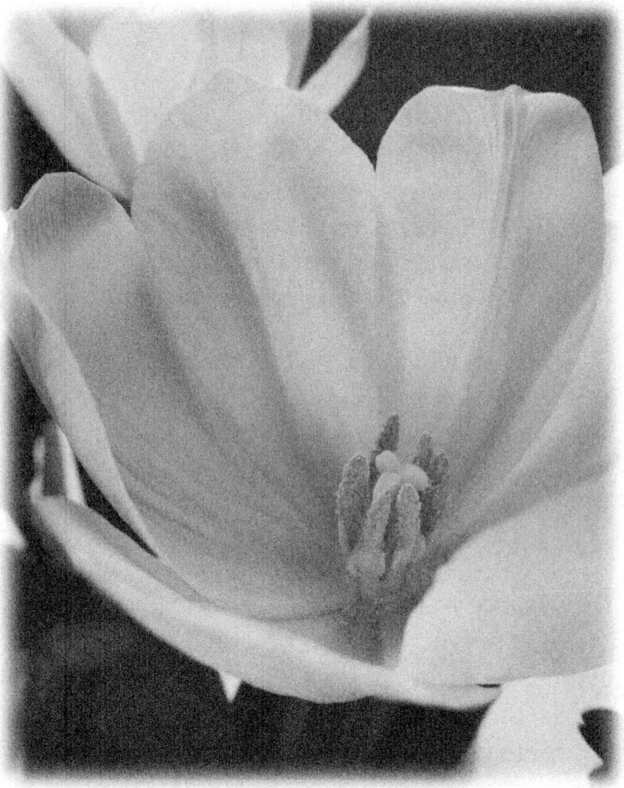

What Do I Do Now?

I'd never seen such beauty before
Never seen such a sweet smile
Eyes that pierced my heart
What do I do - now that I'm in love?

> From your first gaze you entered my heart
> You made me yours from the very start
> What name should I call you -
> when you appear in my dreams?

I've never felt a love such as this
My love, where do we go from here?
You have chosen to enter my life
Give me your name so I may call you?

> This feeling coming from within
> I've never felt this way before
> My love, call me by my name
> My love, may I do the same?

Call me by my name, my love
Call me by my name, my dear
Oh, love of mine, oh love of mine
Let me do the same, let me do the same.

60

Raja And Rani

Raja and Rani have fallen in love
Look at the way they gaze at each other
Their hearts unable to stop skipping
Their minds filled with thoughts so deep
Wondering about their future.

Raja and Rani have fallen in love
Look at how they talk to each other
They can't stop smiling
Raja's never been happier
Rani's never been so content.

Raja and Rani have fallen in love
Look at how they walk with each other
No one can come between them
Their love is so strong a bond
One can't live with the other gone.

Raja and Rani have fallen in love
Look at how they plan together
Their lives are soon to become one
Raja wants to secure his bride
Rani wants to secure her husband.

62

My Heart Kept On Crying

The world kept on turning
The people kept on working
But my heart kept on crying
Unable to forget my love.

What kind of life is this -
without your love by my side?

The wind kept on blowing
The birds kept on singing
But my heart kept on crying
Unable to forget the pain.

What kind of life is this -
without your love by my side?

The flowers kept on blooming
The children kept on playing
But my heart kept on crying
Unable to forget the memories.

My heart won't stop crying -
endures many sleepless nights
My heart can't stop crying -
come rest by my side.

64

A Heart Among Weeping Flowers

When there were flowers blooming - there was you
When there were birds singing - there was you
Now you're gone, what am I to do?
Now you're gone, I'm here alone.

Where have you gone - what did I do?
Who'll fill this heart of mine?

When there were skies blue - there was you
When there was sunshine bright - there was you
Now you're not here, what am I to do?
Now you're gone, I walk alone.

Where have you gone - what did I do?
Who'll play with this heart of mine?

When there was joy and laughter - there was you
When there were warm smiles - there was you
Now you're gone, who do I cry to?
Now you're gone, who'll wipe my tears?

Where have you gone - what did I do?
Who'll mend this heart of mine?

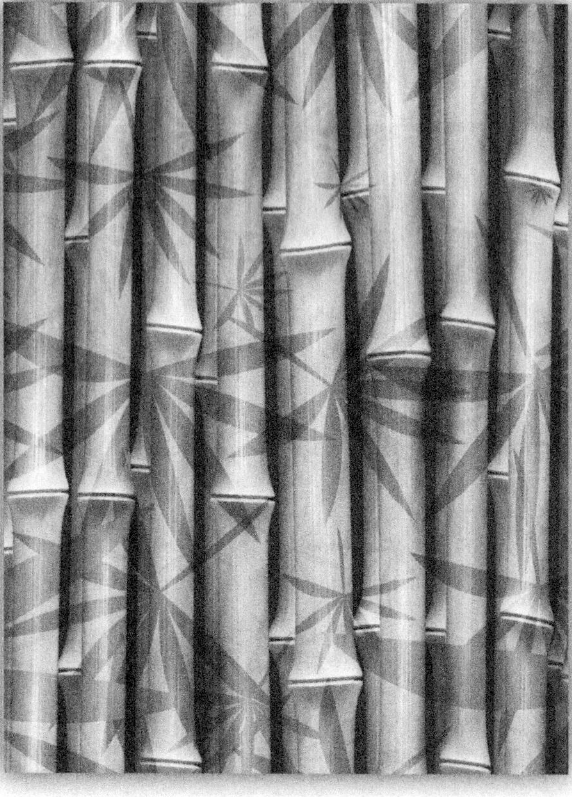

Sunita And Her Love

Oh, my love, at least come to me now
Come, put out the flames in my heart
Pour your cold breath over me
Oh, my love, at least come to me now
After all these months, come put out these flames
Pour your cool breath over me.

Sunita I will be there soon
My thirst can only be quenched by your love
Your lips have made so many promises.

Oh, my love, please come to me now
Put out the flames that you have kindled
Look at the state I am in because of you
Hold me with your ice-cold embrace
I've agreed to all of your wishes
There's nothing I won't do.

Sunita, my wife, I will be there soon
My thirst can only be quenched by your love
Your lips have made so many promises.

Oh, my love, come to me now
Cool the flames of my desire
Pour your cool breath over me.

68

Don't Change Like The Weather

I hope unlike the weather – you won't change
I've given you my life in return for your love
Dreams will change – looks will change
But my love for you will remain the same
I hope unlike the seasons – you won't change
You are my first and final love
No one can compare to you
I want you as much as you desire me
I'll dress you as my bride and marry you
I hope unlike the tides – you won't change
I've given you my life in return for your love
My destination is in your eyes
My Paradise by your side.

70

The Day We Stop Loving Life

The day we stop loving life
Will be the last day of our lives
In our hearts is passion
In our minds, ideas
In our eyes, dreams
The day we stop loving life
Our hearts will die
Our minds will idle
Our eyes turn blind
May we always love life
And may life always love us
The day we stop loving life
Will be the last day of our lives.

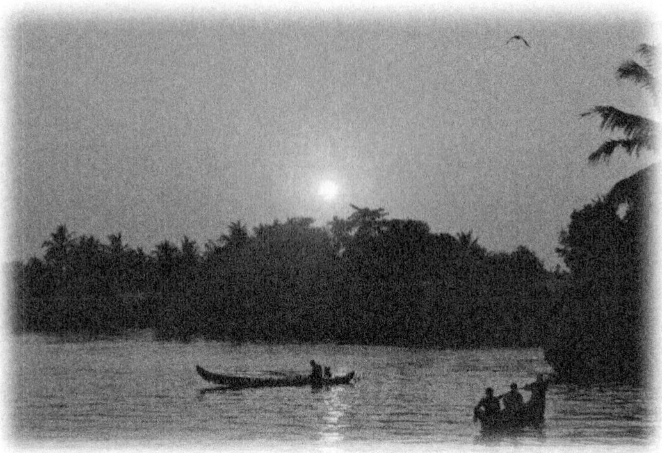

A Day Without Words

There is wisdom in running streams
Guidance in the softest breeze
A lesson in the falling of leaves
And hope in the greening of trees.

74

Slowly

Slowly I fell in love
Slowly I became crazy
Your beauty stole my heart
Meeting you revealed what makes the heart love
Slowly your love touched my soul
Your beauty awoke my heart
We were meant to meet this way
We were destined for each other
This match was made in Heaven.

76

Your Name

I wrote your name on my heart -
Only to wipe off it again.

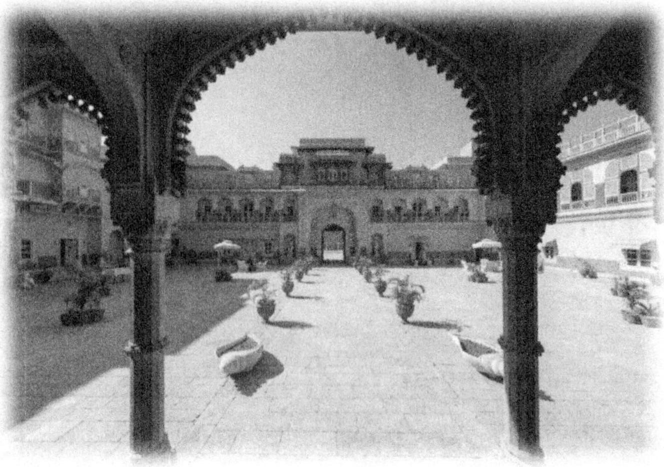

These Are Our Times

These places
These people
These faces
These colours
These clothes
These scents
Today we'll fall in love with the world
Today we'll accept each other's soul
These looks
These stares
These streets
These cultures
These foods
These drinks
These sights
These sounds
These wonders
Tomorrow we'll try something new
Tomorrow we'll find another truth
These good times
These memories
These dreams.

80

Say – Say – Say

Say it with a smile
Say it with a promise
Say it with your heart
Come and say it close to me
Say you're in love
Say you're in love
Say it with shyness
Say it with kindness
As long as you tell me
You're in love
You're in love
My heart flutters on seeing you
It becomes so helpless
I'm so in love with you
So, in love with you
In love with you.

82

A Week Without You
One day without you is cruel
One day without you is eternal
Two days without you is a blur
Two days without you is a nightmare
Three days without you are tragic
Three days without you are manic
Four days without you are lonely
Four days without you are empty
Five days without you are unbearable
Five days without you are regrettable
Six days without you are madness
Six days without you are sadness
Where are you?
Where are?
You
?

Seven days without you are too much
Come back to that I might touch
Y
O
U
.

84

Do You Still Remember?

The promised we'd kept
The dreams we'd made
We said we'd never forget
Do you still remember?
Our days were filled with happiness
Our nights were full of romance
Do you still remember?
We would stay up late
Lost in our own world
We were always together
I would hold you in my arms
Talking about matters of the heart
I always felt so close to you
I was destined for you
Your name was on my lips
Do you still remember?
Yes – I still remember
I fell in love with you at first sight
You made my dreams come true
I saw my future in your eyes
I felt safe in your arms
You still remember?
Yes – I still remember
The promised we'd kept
The dreams we'd made
I still remember.

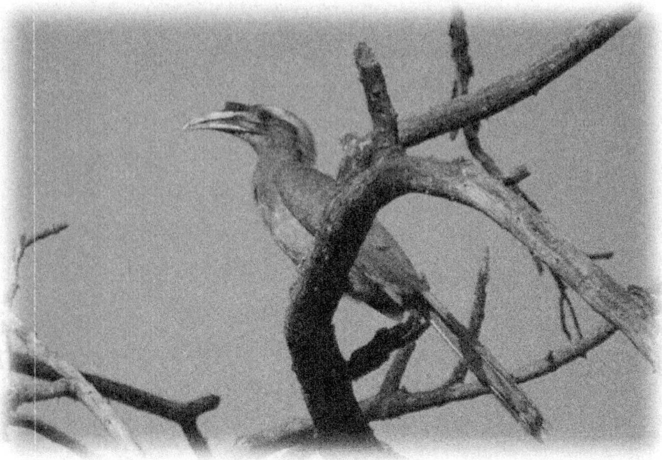

Iron Heart

I've been afraid all my life
I've feared as much as I chose
I've lived and died so many times
I've shed more tears than I can count
Yet I forged a hammer from my iron heart
I broke the locks that kept it down
I feared what might happen to me
Yet I found freedom and love
Freedom and a love of life.

88

My Dear Life

I've lived as much as I can
I've feared as much as I will
I've fallen in love with life
I'm as free as my voice.

90

Tell Me

Tell me how you spent your day?
Tell me how you spent your night?
Be honest, did you think of me?
To be honest, sometimes I did
Sometimes I forgot about you
Could you live without me?
I couldn't live without you
I couldn't live with you.

92

Your Face

I saw you face in the moon and stars
When I fell in love with you
Our hears became one home to share
Our dreams all came true.

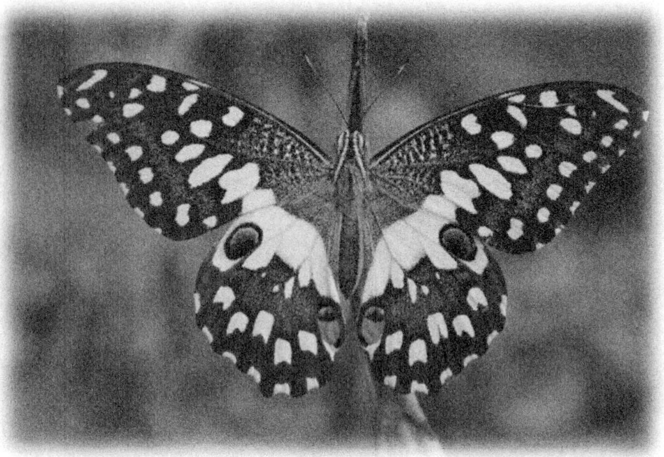

I Don't Need It

Why do I need drugs when I have good health?
Why do I need alcohol when I have great friends?
Why do I need wealth when I have glorious youth?

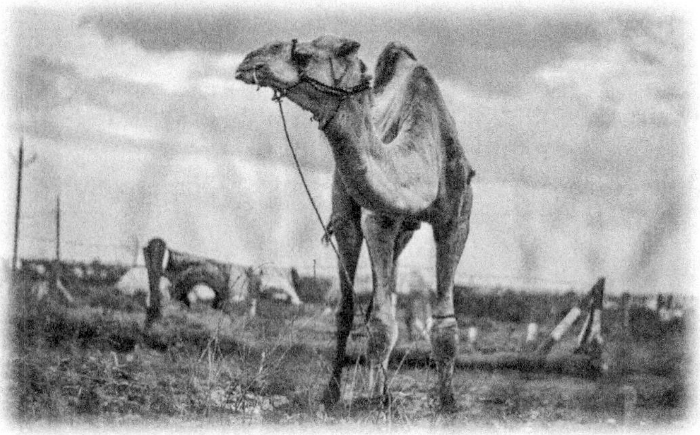

The Trials of Life

There are trials for the single, the married, the separated and the divorced.

There are tribulations for the rich, the poor, the homeless and the housed.

There are hardships for the weak, the strong, the healthy and the sick.

There are money troubles for the employed and the unemployed.

There are fears for those with children and those without.

There are battles for every man, woman, boy and girl.

There are no easy paths in this demanding world.

98

I'll Be Your Vice

I'll be your cigarette
I'll be your glass of wine
You won't need rom-coms
You won't need comfort food
I'll cook you lunch and supper
I'll be your spring and summer
You won't need your dating app
You won't need to avoid weddings.

100

Useless

This is the first time my heart has proven so useless –
If I didn't know any better - I'd say it's fallen in love.

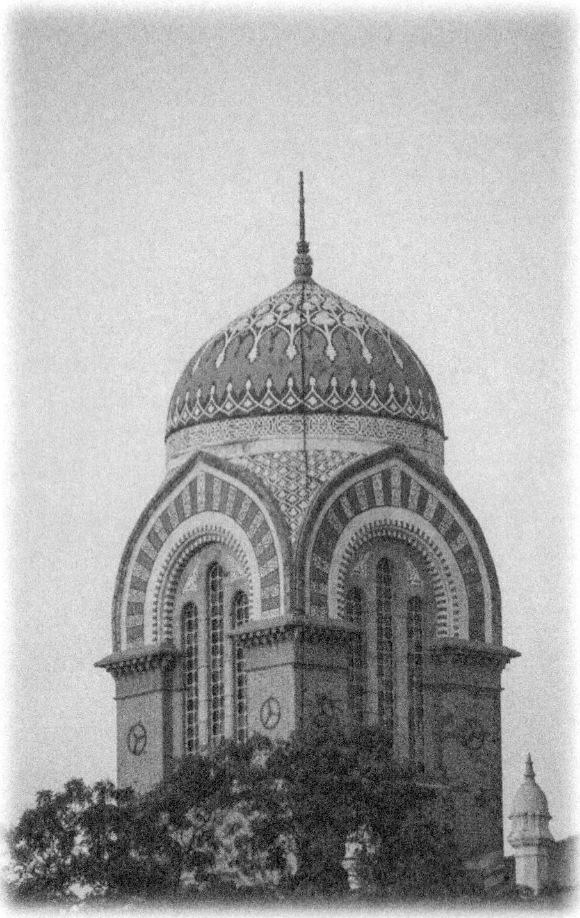

Away

I will go far away from you -
Just to know how it feels.

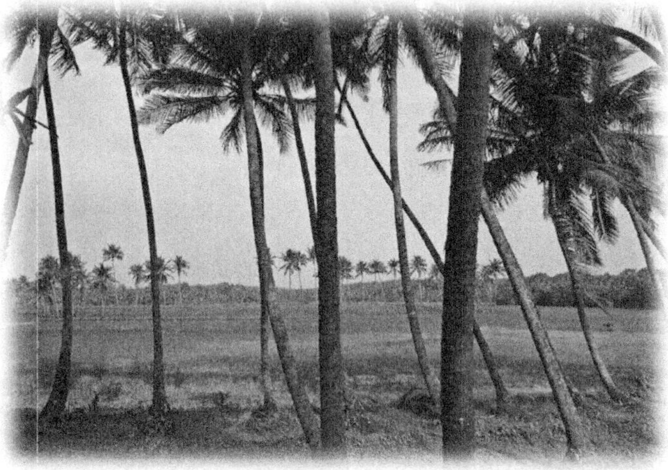

Trust

Just fall in love –
Then trust and wait
Don't leave it too late.

106

Not Twice

I need your love
Not one, not twice
But a hundred times.

108

Dreams

You are in my dreams –
You are in my thoughts
Why do you trouble me?

110

Eternal

There is beauty external and internal
The eternal will weather and fade
But the internal will always remain.

112

Still

You wear no jewellery
You wear no make-up
You wear no fine clothes
Yet you are still beautiful.

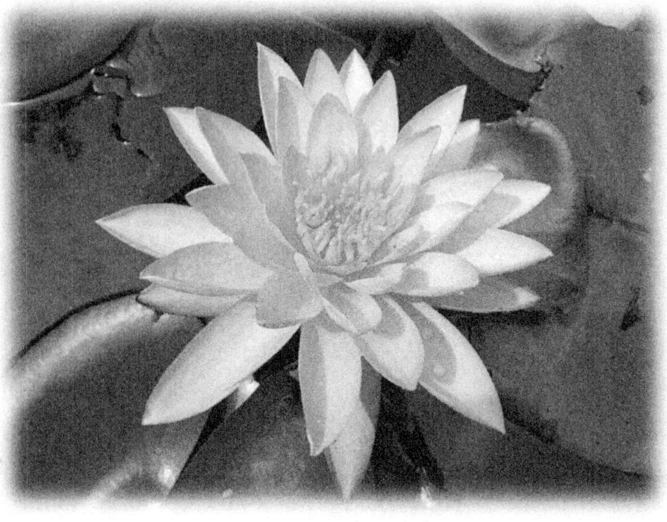

Rain

I fell for her like yesterday's rain
Today I woke heartache again.

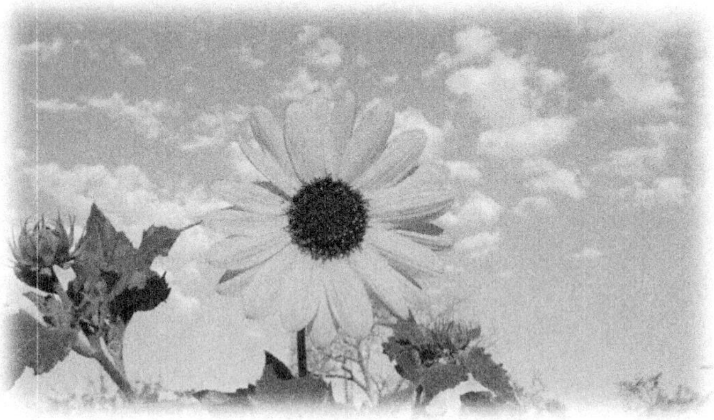

I'd Fallen

I stopped to think
Rain began to fall
Time stood still
I'd fallen in love.

The sky darkened
The night crept in
Time stood still
I'd fallen in love.

The cold bit me
My path closed
Time stood still
I'd fallen in love.

My heart raced
New feelings grew
Time moved on
I'd fallen in love.

118

I Love You

I've forgotten everything
I can't remember anything
Yet there's one I can't forget
I can't forget that you love me.

You've forgotten everything
You can't remember anything
Yet there's one thing you can't forget
That I love you.

120

You're A Part Of My Daily Life

From the clothes you wear
To the colour of your hair
You're part of my daily life.

From the friends you choose
To the style of your shoes
You're part of my daily life.

From the colour of your skin
To whether you lose or win
You're part of my daily life.

From the smell of your perfume
To success or ruin
You're part of my daily life.

From being married or single
Whether you choose to mingle
You're part of my daily life.

122

Fragrance

Your fragrance fills my home
Your eyes in me cause a storm
This ship won't sail far from port.

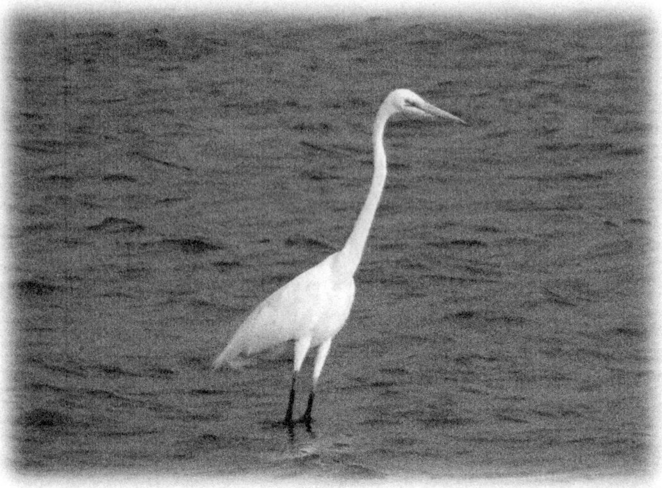

Unhide

In your eyes lies the spark that ignites my heart
Nothing is hidden, nothing I hide
In your eyes lies my future.

126

Faults

When you meet *the one* -
Your faults
Your weaknesses
and your mistakes
Will disappear.

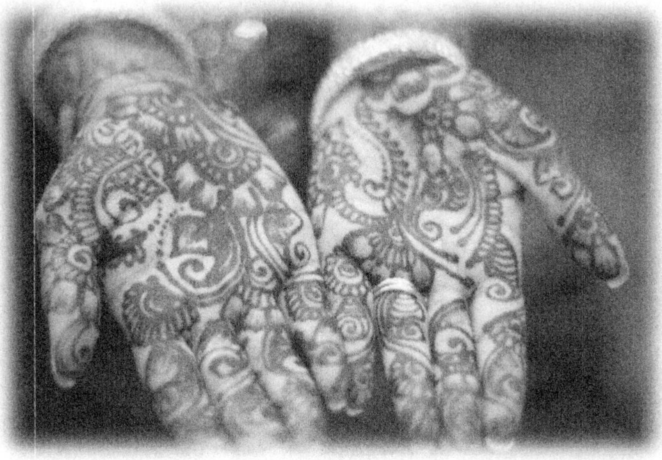

Nothing's The Same

Same house – but it feels bigger
Same fridge – but such little food
Same wardrobe – only fewer clothes
Same sink – but fewer dishes to wash
Same car – only a different route
Same television – only more to watch
Same telephone – only fewer calls
Same guy – only without the girl
Nothing's the same.

130

Flowers

Like flowers our love spread
Your joy was my joy
Your dream was my dream
What else did we need?

132

Thanks To You

I'm not a poet -
but I learnt poetry on seeing you.
I'm not a romantic -
but I learnt romance on meeting you.
I'm not an artist -
but I learnt to paint on viewing you.
I'm not a lover -
but I learnt to love in your presence.
I'm not a traveller -
but I learnt to travel with you.
I'm all of the above -
Thanks to you.

134

Deep

Without destination –
The oar paddles the lake
Causing an upheaval in my heart.

136

Star Crossed

When He created hearts
He created them in two parts
and wrote a name on each part
One Romeo - one Juliet.

138

The Night A Meeting Occurred

Last night I met someone –
Last night a meeting occurred
Some words were exchanged – but
What I wanted to say was left unspoken.

What did you want to say?

I wanted to say, I'd fallen in love
I wanted to say, my heart was stolen
I wanted to ask you –
When will we meet again?

Last night I heard some words – but
What I wanted to hear was left untold.

What did you want to hear?

That you'd fallen in love too
That I'd also stolen your heart
I wanted you to ask me –
When will I see you again?

140

In The Ticking of My Watch

I can't stop thinking about your words
You're still alive in my heart – somewhere
Some place I can't see you – can't touch you
Wherever I live – you'll be there by my side
I'll hear your heart in the ticking of my watch
Even though we're very far apart.

I still recall the days we spent together
I hear your heart in the ticking of my watch
Wherever you are - I'll be there with you
I can't stop thinking about your words
I can't forget the memories we made
We're apart, but still together
In the ticking of my watch.

142

It Takes A Third To Unite Lovers
I don't know what you want –
You said you never understood me
It takes a third to unite lovers.
I've been wanting to contact you –
I don't know if you want any contact
It takes a third to unite lovers.
I was confused and needed to get away –
You kept saying I never loved you
It takes a third to unite lovers.
I don't know if you miss me –
You don't know that I miss you
It takes a third to unite lovers.
I live in hope that we'll unite someday –
I hope you'll feel the same way
It takes a third to unite lovers.

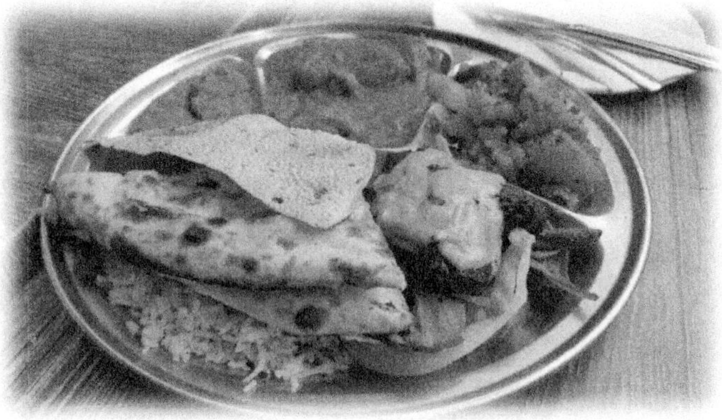

Broken Pieces
I'll pick up pieces of broken Moon
I'll sweep up fallen rays of Sun
I'll remove piercing stars
To you I'll return
To you
I'll
Return
.

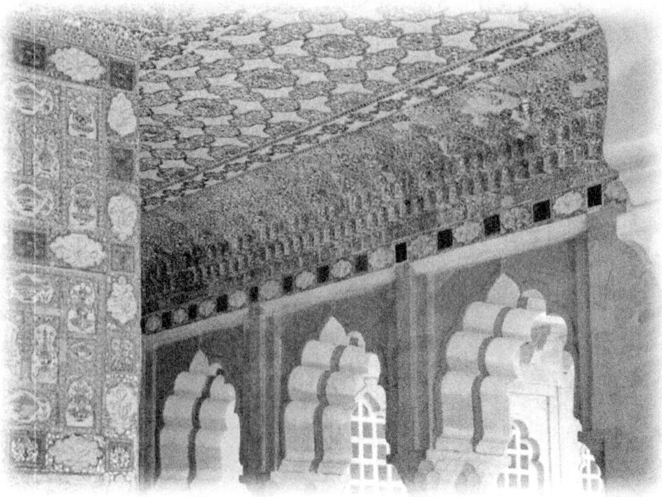

Hide

Hide yourself from the Sun –
Or you'll outshine it.
Hide yourself from the flowers –
Or you'll put them to shame.
Hide yourself from the Moon –
Or we risk losing it.

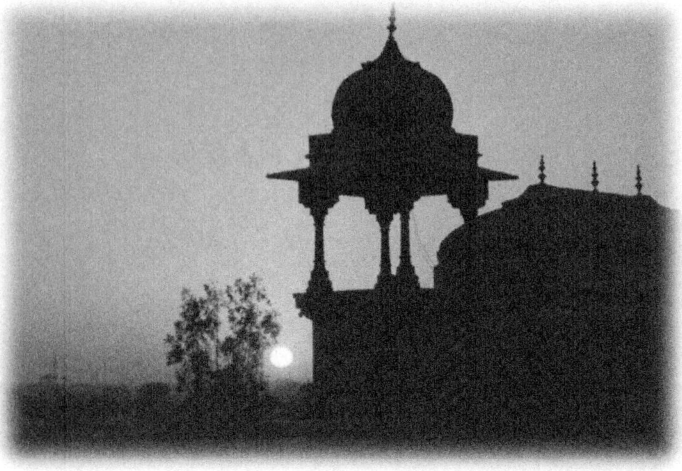

THE END

More books by W.M.Aslam

Poetry

Graphic Heart Vocabulary

Eastern Heart Vocabulary

Rhyming Vice

Fifteen Decibel

Childsworth

Fiction

Toby Glass and the Terracotta Army

The Life and Death of Danny McGhee

The Very Strange Tale of Mr. Straw

Scott McNally's Mystery

Dawn: The Girl Who Talks To Ghosts

Beneath My Bed

Four Charming Tales For Children